THE JOY OF DISCIPLING

E. STANLEY OTT

THE JOY OF DISCIPLING

*Friend
with
Friend,
Heart with
Heart*

**Lamplighter
Books** Grand Rapids,
Michigan
Zondervan Publishing House

Also by E. Stanley Ott, *The Vibrant Church*

The Joy of Discipling
Copyright © 1989 by E. Stanley Ott

Lamplighter Books are published by Zondervan Publishing House
1415 Lake Drive, S.E., Grand Rapids, Michigan 49506

Library of Congress Cataloging-in-Publication Data

Ott, E. Stanley, 1948–
    The Joy of discipling / by E. Stanley Ott.
      p. cm.
    "Lamplighter books."
    ISBN 0-310-24821-3
    1. Evangelistic work. 2. Fellowship—Religious aspects—
Christianity. I. Title.
BV3790.085 1989
253–dc20   89–16426
                                                    CIP

Edited by John Sloan, Mary McCormick
Designed by Louise Bauer

Printed in the United States of America

89 90 91 92 93 94 / ML / 10 9 8 7 6 5 4 3 2 1

Dedicated with love to Jim Tozer.
Being with him is a privilege and a joy.

CONTENTS

Come with me, walk with me,
Run with me, fly with me.
We will roam the Father's land together.
—KEN MEDEMA

FOREWORD

In the first church that I was called to pastor, Coalinga, California, many of the women members urged me to "get my husband in the church." In responding to this request I grew into a ministry with men, many of whom were oil workers. Very soon it became obvious as I called on them while they worked on the rigs, that they could not be disturbed while they were operating the heavy machinery lest distraction cause an accident. Usually

I waited until they had noticed me, finished the task on which they were working, and invited conversation. Actually this was true in stores, offices, and shops as well. If businessmen were busy, I waited until it was convenient for them to give me a few minutes. Without realizing it, I was learning a fundamental in ministry—that is, adjust to the convenience of others and submit to their agenda.

There were no books on "discipleship" in those days. In fact, one rarely heard the word. I decided to study the Gospels inductively (the only method, I'm convinced) looking for one thing: how did Jesus relate to people? How did He minister to men? The first principle became apparent early in the study—one could not develop a method on the basis of Jesus' style. He treated each person differently. Each person was addressed with respect and love according to that person's situation at the time of contact. I began to realize that any one method, however wise and thoughtful, could not be used indiscriminately. To do so was to be manipulative in some degree in a way that violated personality and imposed my agenda, whatever it was, on the person being contacted. It made people "its" to be worked on, rather than persons to be with, to love, to respect and serve.

In the course of this study of the Gospels, Mark 3:14 became definitive and prescriptive for my ministry. The big word became *with*. Previously I had ministered to or at people. They were objects to fulfill my mission, my agenda. Now they became persons to be with, to be heeded, to be listened to, to hear and to love. People were to be responded to where *they* were, not where I was.

Two other texts became definitive in my pilgrimage: Mark 4:34 and John 15:15. While He was with them, Jesus "explained everything" to His disciples and shared with them "all that the Father gave Him." Little by little over a period of years there emerged a simple definition of the ministry into which God was leading me. I was to "be with people at their convenience in terms of time and place without an agenda." Their need in their circumstances as illuminated by the Holy Spirit became my agenda. I had no agenda except to love as God enabled me. And because love works only on contact, to love I must be with them.

Stan Ott has captured the essence of the significance and strategy (if such it be) of "with-ness" and carried it far beyond and into greater depths than ever I have. At a time when much of the evangelical approach is based on its agenda rather than on the needs and circumstances of those being served, this book is a blessed respite and motivator. In their uniqueness and personhood, people are best served by one's being with them rather than by doing something for them and talking to or at them. This does not mean that we do not do something for them or talk with them. It does mean that we are with them enough to discover, as the Spirit guides, their need in the circumstances in which they find themselves, so that we may respond in God's love and with the wisdom He gives us in that situation.

Richard C. Halverson

PREFACE

There is no greater joy than being "with people"—growing as friends as we grow in Christ. The with-me principle is a simple expression of the profound biblical truth that God is a God *with* us. He invites us to be with Him. He promises to be with us. We, in turn, ask people to be with us to share fellowship with each other and with God Himself.

Dick Halverson focused on the significance of

"with" early in his ministry. God has used this simple idea to encourage countless persons to grow in Christ with Dick. I first learned of the with-me concept from Chuck Miller who practices it in an incomparable way. Both of these men have taught me a great deal and it has been a God-given joy and privilege to know them.

I am grateful for the privilege of sharing life with many friends whose names appear on these pages. Their impact on my life is beyond measure. I am particularly thankful for the many suggestions of my wife, Ann Marie, and for Susan Dunsmore who has patiently typed this manuscript.

Chapter 1

THE JOY OF DISCIPLING

I love the word "with" because I am convinced it is one of the most significant words in the whole Bible. The with-ness of the Christian faith is one of its most exciting dimensions. In fact, with-ness is crucial for life to be complete, fulfilling, and joyful.

I'll never forget one summer vacation a few years ago. Ann Marie and I and the kids spent a marvelous week with my parents in Virginia. As we backed out of their driveway and began the long ride home to Indiana, I was awash with a sense of loss that lasted for a hundred miles.

I had been away from home more than ten years, was married-with-children, and happily pursuing my career. Although I had experienced normal feelings of homesickness when leaving home in the past, somehow this sense of loss was deeper, more profound. Was something wrong with me? No. I was simply deeply in touch with how much I loved those people and how much I wanted to be near them. We have a need to be with those we love—to be near them—to share life with them.

After the apostle Paul had collected a gift from the churches of Macedonia, he sailed south to take it to the Christians in Jerusalem. On the way, he stopped at Miletus, a small town on the coast of Asia Minor, and sent for the elders of the church of Ephesus. Paul had spent three years in Ephesus, building a church with such impact that its witness had gone all across Asia Minor. In Acts 20 we read how Paul, when the elders reached him, gave them a farewell speech in which he shared his philosophy of ministry.

I find that a highly significant part of the whole event occurred after his speech. Paul told these men that he would never see them again. When they knelt on the beach to pray, they wept and hugged and kissed one another. For Paul, ministry was far more than a teaching of content. They had become close personal friends. Their lives were melded one with another. *With-ness is essential to real relationships.* Significantly, when Luke tells how these elders fell upon Paul's neck, he uses the same expression he used to describe the prodigal son's father who fell upon his returning son's neck and kissed him. There is great joy in being "with" those we love.

I remember when our best man, Wayne Helmer, had finished his Ph.D. at Purdue University. We gathered in a small group Bible study that had met for years, and Wayne shared that message from Acts with us. When he described the part about Paul and the elders of Ephesus weeping as they said good-bye, I could scarcely control my own emotion. After the prayer time was over, Wayne joined me outside and we wept together.

There is a deep need within us to be with—to be near people we love and to share life at its deepest levels. The concept of "being with" can be a nice theory, a new principle, an interesting idea, but it means far more than that. It is real relationships. It is being friends of the heart. It is sharing life at such deep levels that if you move or the other person leaves, you weep.

Life can be shallow as we bounce off others in simple social contact. When we understand what it really means to say "God is with us" and to know what it is to share life with other people in friendship and discipleship, we receive one of the great treasures of life.

"With" in Scripture

As the concept of "with" took hold of my life, I was stunned by the significance of with-ness throughout Scripture. When God spoke to Moses out of the burning bush and said, "I will send you to Pharaoh," Moses said to God, "Who am I, that I should go to Pharaoh, and that I should bring the sons of Israel out of Egypt?" God replies, "Certainly I will be with you" (Exod. 3:11–12). This was an incredible promise.

Although Moses was yet to identify this God, we learn in Genesis that He is El Shaddai—God Almighty. This is the God of power who created the world and showed His incredible power to Abraham, Isaac, and Jacob. We know that God was saying, "I, the God of infinite and literal power, will be by your side." "With" becomes the crucial word, for by using that word God guarantees to Moses His presence and His power.

Forty years later when Moses passes from the scene, having known God's presence in the most personal way, the baton of leadership passes to Moses' right-hand man, Joshua. Imagine the responsibility of replacing the first great leader of over a million people! When we take on a new task, a new project, a new responsibility, fear is a normal emotion. We fear failure. We fear criticism. We fear our own inadequacy. God, knowing of that fear, spoke to Joshua, "Have I not commanded you? Be strong and courageous! Do not tremble or be dismayed, for the LORD your God is with you wherever you go"

(Josh. 1:9). As with Moses and Joshua, God, the God of power, guarantees to be with you.

As we move through the Old Testament, we come to David, a man after God's own heart—and the beautiful Twenty-third Psalm. In the three thousand years since that psalm was written, people have faced difficulty countless times, and David's words have offered the greatest comfort imaginable: "Even though I walk through the valley of the shadow of death, I fear no evil; for Thou art with me" (Ps. 23:4). What an affirmation! For us to know that God is with us is a "confession of faith" and one of the most comforting thoughts we can have.

Continuing our journey through Scripture, in Matthew 1 we find a quote from the prophet Isaiah: "Behold, the virgin shall be with child, and shall bear a Son, and they shall call His name Immanuel," which, translated, means "God with us" (Isa. 7:14; Matt. 1:23). Incredibly, the very name of Jesus Christ is "God with us." Being "with" is so much a part of God's very nature that He named the Messiah with a preposition!

In the marvelous Great Commission that concludes the gospel according to Matthew, Jesus commands us to go unto all the world. He concludes by saying, "Lo, I am with you." God's very nature in the Old Testament is revealed to be "with." He sends His Son whom He has named "God With Us" to be truly present to us. Before Jesus goes to His Father, He promises that He will not leave us alone and promises to send a Helper to be with us (John 14:16–18).

It is the great desire of Jesus Christ to have His people next to Him. It is not only evident in Matthew but throughout the New Testament.

For example, Jesus promises that "where I am, there you may be also" (John 14:3). In His great prayer to the Father Jesus says, "Father, I desire that they also, whom Thou hast given Me, be with Me . . ." (John 17:24). Paul tells us how God "made us alive together with Christ (by grace you have been saved), and raised us up with Him and seated us with Him in the heavenly *places* in Christ Jesus" (Eph. 2:5, 6). Jesus Christ is with us in the most personal, immediate sense possible. He is among us now by means of the Spirit, and one day we will join Him to behold His glory and to rejoice in fellowship of His company.

The power of the presence of Jesus Christ among us extends into our relationships with others. As we grow as disciples of Jesus Christ, He enables us to grow deep in personal friendship and sends us to do His work in the people with whom we share life.

Tom Meade and his wife, Janet, moved into town to start a new carwashing business. They bought a house not far from our church. Because of its convenience, they began to worship with us each Sunday. Janet came from a Christian family and had a deep sense of what it meant to grow as a disciple of Jesus Christ. Tom had little understanding of what the Christian faith was all about, but he supported Janet and accompanied her and their family to church.

The Meades joined a small Bible study led by Bob and Mary LaTurner that met every Wednesday evening. Bob and Mary quickly sensed the depth of Janet's faith in Christ and that Tom was unfamiliar with spiritual things. They began to build a close friendship with the Meades, and other members of the small group began to invite the Meades over socially. In the warmth of the group, Tom began to feel the freedom to ask personal and spiritual questions such as, "Who is Jesus Christ?" and "What does it mean to be committed to Him?" Toward the end of the group's meeting one evening, Tom said, "I have decided to ask Jesus into my life and I would like to do it with you." There in the living room of their home, he asked Jesus Christ to come into his life.

I have never seen a person grow spiritually as rapidly as Tom did. We became friends as we jogged together each morning and shared in a number of activities at the church. Time with members of his small group and other Christian men was rapidly building Tom into an articulate, loving, Christian man when suddenly great pain came into his life. Tom's lower back was causing him agony, yet repeated tests in many hospitals could find no cause.

One day as I was sitting in a graduate class at Purdue University, there was a knock at the classroom door. I was asked to come immediately to the hospital where Tom had just undergone exploratory surgery. Janet said to me, "They found cancer in the pancreas. Would you go into his room with me to tell him?" "Of course," I replied.

The two of us entered the room where Tom was lying on his side in bed. As we approached, he said, "Hi, Stan. The news isn't good, is it?"

I said, "No, Tom, it's not good."

He said, "It's cancer, isn't it?"

"Yes," I answered. "It's cancer."

A pained expression came over Tom's face, then he rolled over onto his back. Staring straight up at the ceiling, he began to speak slowly, firmly, "Jesus is Lord, Jesus is Lord, Jesus is Lord, Jesus is Lord, Jesus is *Lord!*"

The hair on the back of my neck began to prickle. I realized that Tom was no longer speaking to me. He was confessing his faith in Jesus Christ. The time he had shared with the LaTurners and other people in his small group had led him to an absolutely genuine confession of faith in Jesus Christ. That discipleship brought tremendous strength to Tom in a very difficult moment. In the year that Tom was given to live, I watched him minister to his family and lead both his mother and one of his dear friends to Jesus Christ. Tom not only met Christ through the fellowship of a few Christian friends, but he became an "apostle"—one who is sent to lead others to Christ and to build them in His way.

The joy of discipling is friend with friend, heart

with heart. *In the process of sharing life, of growing as friends, we can meet Christ together and face some of the difficult moments of life together.* At the same time, we can send one another as "apostles" to do His work and to be His witnesses in our families, in our Christian fellowship, and in our place of work.

Whatever your own situation in life may be, whatever circumstances you face, however fearful, concerned, or anxious you may be—He is with you. Put your trust in Jesus Christ. To lean upon Him as the Rock is to know that He is immediately present with you from this moment and forever.

Discussion Questions

1. Recall a time when you were separated from someone you loved. What was the occasion? How did you feel? What do those feelings tell you about the importance of "with"?
2. When did you first become aware that God is with you? What were you doing then?
3. Look up John 14:1–6, Psalm 23, and Isaiah 43:1–7. What do you learn about God's with-ness in Scripture?
4. What other biblical passages are you aware of that teach God is with you?
5. Faith in Jesus Christ is the key to knowing that God is with you. Can you say with confidence that you have committed your life to Jesus Christ? If not, you can do so immediately by going to Him in prayer.

Chapter 2

LOVE IS BEING WITH

The concept that God is with us is one of the most potent, life-changing, and significant ideas that we can ever know. Countless hymns and poems and stories have been written around the affirmation, "Thou art with me!" Of course, the bond that brings God and people together and holds them in with-ness is the bond of love.

Love impels us to be near one another. Super Bowl XXIII pitted two great teams, the San Francisco

49ers and the Cincinnati Bengals, against each other. Sam Wyche, the coach of the Bengals, and Bill Walsh, coach of the 49ers, are close friends (Sam worked as an assistant coach for Bill for a number of years). The game was not decided until the final minutes of play when the 49ers finally pulled ahead to stay. The game was so close and exciting that the winners were sure to be exhilarated and the losers badly disappointed.

Following the game, amid the very confusing swarm of players and television cameramen, the two head coaches met one another midfield. Typically, coaches shake hands briefly, then quickly turn to be with their own teams. Yet surprisingly, Bill Walsh and Sam Wyche walked together across the entire length of the football field, their arms around each other's shoulder.

NBC sportscaster, Bob Costas, interviewed Bill Walsh after the game and asked, "Were you able to exchange words of any kind?"

"Oh, yes," replied Bill, "we left the field together. I love him very much."

"What was said—if you would share that?" asked Costas.

"Well," said Bill Walsh, "we care for each other." These two men, one in joy, the other in pain after being locked in intense competition, yet were drawn together in the midst of great confusion and mixed emotion. Love calls us to draw near.

Much has been written about the many words for love found in the original languages in which the

Bible was written. There are two incredibly powerful words that show how God's love means He is the "with" God. The first word is an Old Testament word *hesed*. To many it is the most important word in the Old Testament. It has so many shades of profound meaning that the various English translations tend to use different phrases to express its meaning. For example, the Revised Standard Version speaks of God's steadfast love, the New American Standard Version of God's lovingkindness, and the King James Bible speaks of mercy.

Hesed is a word that describes God's faithful love—His covenant love. As God draws us into a relationship with Him, He makes a covenant with us, a holy agreement, a sacred promise in which He guarantees to give us His *hesed*. It is God saying, "*Hesed* means I will never remove my love from you!"

Hesed means no matter how I fail, no matter how I am faithless, God will never withdraw His love from me. If you have put your faith in Christ and entered into the new covenant, then *hesed* is yours. His mercy is yours. His love has not been removed nor will it ever be removed no matter who you are or what you have done. His forgiveness in Christ is complete.

Hesed means God is with you and He will never leave you. As Hebrews 13:5 quotes, "I will never desert you, nor will I ever forsake you."

The concept of *hesed* in the Old Testament finds expression in the New Testament in the word for "mercy." However, another New Testament word for love that corresponds to the concept of *hesed* is that of *agape*. *Agape* love is unconditional love. It comes from God to us no matter what we have done, no matter what we are like. Whereas *hesed* love suggests that God will never take back His love once he gives it, *agape* suggests God will always give His love.

Agape love comes looking for you, finds you no matter where you are, no matter what you've done, no matter how you feel. As you respond to that *agape* love through faith in Jesus Christ, the *hesed* of God means that love will never be withdrawn. The *agape* love of God courts. He seeks you out and invites you to put your trust in Jesus Christ. The *hesed* love of God keeps. He keeps covenant. He keeps faithfulness. He will never leave you.

In the New Testament we make the exciting discovery that God's commitment to us is to be expressed in our commitment to others. As we practice *agape*, we are impelled to be involved in the lives of others, to be near them no matter what they are like. By our *hesed* we show our own covenant commitment to the people in our lives, showing that nothing will ever cause us to withdraw our love. As God is faithful to us, so are we faithful to others. We grow in Christian discipleship as we come to understand the implications of words like *hesed* and *agape*. In obedience to the apostle Peter's command, "Fervently love one another from the heart" (1 Peter 1:22).

Sun

There are several Greek words for the idea of "with" that are translated "with" in our English Bibles. However, there's one Greek word for "with" that is frequently used, and that has a very wonderful meaning. That Greek word is the word *sun* (pronounced "soon"). *Sun* is simply translated as "with" but it can mean much more than simply being together physically. At its deepest level, *sun* means shared life, a common bond. For me to grow with you in the sense of *sun* means that our relationship would begin at a shallow level but as we grow more and more in our relationship, will move from acquaintance to good friend to deep friend. When we are with each other in the deep sense of *sun*, it means covenant commitment, that all that I have is yours, all that you have is mine. We share life at its most significant level.

Interestingly, the closest synonym to this concept of with is the Greek word for fellowship, *koinonia*. *Koinonia* means shared life, having the common bond. To share in fellowship, to have *koinonia* at its most basic level, is "to be with."

Now the fascinating thing about the Greek word *sun* is the way it is used as a prefix on other words. For example, Paul speaks of Epaphroditus as "my brother and fellow worker and fellow soldier" (Phil. 2:25). In the Greek it is "Epaphroditus, my brother," and *sun* worker and *sun* soldier. Frequently when you see the English word "fellow," or "joint," or "co-" used as prefixes, the Greek language is using the concept of "with." The use of *sun* literally saturates the New Testament, indicating the overwhelming emphasis of Scripture on this essential concept.

When John writes his first epistle, he says that our fellowship is "with us, and indeed our fellowship is with the Father, and with His Son Jesus Christ" (1 John 1:3). The sense is that we share life together and with the triune God at the deepest possible levels. Every spiritual blessing God offers is ours. All that we have is His. All that I have is yours. All that you have is mine. This is not to suggest I will take what is yours but rather we will serve each other with what God has given us.

Discussion Questions

1. Would it be appropriate to call "love" the verb of with-ness? Why?
2. "With" means more than simply being in the same room. As *koinonia* or shared life, what are some of the deeper implications of life "with one another"?

Chapter 3

HEART WITH HEART

One of the most delightful of New Testament words is the word "paraclete." Perhaps it is best understood by the New American Standard translation, "one called alongside to help." "Paraclete" has the sense of alongsideness. The prefix "para" means next to each other. From it we get the word "parallel" (two lines next to each other), parachute (the chute and the person next to each other), parachurch (an organization next to the church), and so on.

Yet "paraclete "in the New Testament means more than simply being alongside—it is alongside *to help*. Frequently "paraclete" is translated into the English language with one of the three words "encourager," "comforter," or "exhorter." For me to "paraclete" you is to encourage you or to comfort you or to exhort you. Each of the English words has a slightly different sense, yet they combine together into the one concept of one person paracleting or building another person in life.

"Paraclete" is one of the key New Testament terms for the ministry of God in our own lives and our ministry one to another. Typically, it is the Holy Spirit who receives credit for being The Paraclete, and yet a study of the New Testament reveals the concept of "paraclete" to be one of the basic attributes of the whole triune God.

In 2 Corinthians 1:3 we read about the God and Father of our Lord Jesus Christ, the Father of mercies and God of all comfort. The Greek word for comfort is "paraclete." God the Father is a paraclete. The Father comes alongside to help.

Then, in 1 John 2:1 we read that we have an advocate with the Father, Jesus Christ the Righteous. The Greek word for "advocate" is "paraclete." Jesus Christ is a paraclete. The Son comes alongside to help.

Finally we read in John 14:26 about the helper, the Holy Spirit whom the Father will send in My name. The Greek word for helper is "paraclete." The Spirit comes alongside to help.

The whole Trinity is paraclete! Although it is true that each person of the Trinity expresses that paracleting, helping ministry differently—the Father comforting, the Son advocating, the Spirit helping—yet those English words overlap in meaning. We learn from the New Testament that the triune God is paraclete in all three persons, and discover what is evident in all of Scripture: God is a helper. He is The Paraclete. Read Psalm 146 to see how clearly the Hebrew people saw God as the helper.

Essential to the life of discipleship is the concept that just as God is paraclete, so we, too, as His people, are to be paraclete. We come alongside to be "with" and so to help.

Several years ago *Sports Illustrated* magazine carried a marvelous story about Don Shula, coach of the Miami Dolphins. When Shula was playing football in college, his roommate was another player, Carl Taseff. Don and Carl played together in college, then went on to play ten years together with the Baltimore Colts. Continuing as roommates, they were close friends. Finally Don left the Colts, and the two friends were separated. Soon afterward Carl was involved in a terrible accident. His nose was crushed, he was unconscious for three weeks, he lost fifty pounds, and his life hung in the balance. As Carl began to regain consciousness, he became aware through blurry vision of a figure kneeling in his room praying. The person was Don Shula. Don was a paraclete coming alongside to help, to encourage and to comfort—to pray for his friend.

As God is a paraclete for us so we become paracletes for one another as we come alongside to help.

For a week of inspiration and study, the Presbyterian Congress on Renewal brought to Dallas thousands of Presbyterians concerned about bringing renewal to the church. Jim Tozer and I had the privilege of sharing lunch together with Bob Munger, former pastor of the great University Presbyterian Church in Seattle, and now pastor emeritus of the First Presbyterian Church of Berkeley.

Bob has given his life to the building of people by discipling. In fact, his seminar at the Congress was on that very subject. We sat in the farthest corner of a huge cafeteria, and were interrupted at least every three minutes by someone who wanted to hug Bob and express love. After lunch I followed him out to the bus stop and rode with him on the way to our hotels. Once again people talked to him every few minutes no matter where we were or what we were doing. It was the greatest possible confirmation that discipling builds loving relationships.

It wasn't until I returned home that I learned something of the secret to this man's incredible network of friends. John McCreight, an associate at a neighboring Presbyterian church, heard me say that I had met Bob Munger in Dallas. John told me that he had taken a class from Bob while at Fuller Seminary, and had grown to know him personally. On one occasion Bob shared how he was counseling a man who was facing the toughest crisis of his life. Bob said, in effect, "I do not know the answer to your problem my friend, but what I do have is a heart to place alongside your heart." This is what it means to be a paraclete, to be "with"—the sense of sharing life at its deepest levels. We place our hearts alongside each other. Discipleship is friend with friend, heart with heart, loving Jesus Christ and loving one another.

The concept of the paraclete becomes even more meaningful when we consider the question, "Who has been a paraclete in my own life?" Who are the people who have come along your side, in your time of need—people who affirm and build and encourage you, whose faith has sustained you, and whose love has been there when you needed it? Wayne Helmer and I became close friends while graduate students at Purdue University. We both entered the Christian faith about the same time and were doing graduate research in the same room. We began to meet each week to study the Bible together and simply share what God was doing in our own lives. We grew in our faith, and we became close friends. Whenever I had a problem or a need or whenever Wayne had one, we would go into the photographic darkroom of the laboratory. A little red light on the outside of the darkroom was the signal that indicated that the door was not to be opened because photographs were being developed. We would turn that little light on to gain privacy, and then go into the room to pray with each other about an immediate problem we were facing. Repeatedly we discovered that God was in our relationship, that He received the problem we were lifting to Him, and that He provided new strength and direction for our lives. We became paracletes for one another.

Discipling is the process by which we encourage and enable another person to grow as a disciple of Jesus Christ. If prayer is the first step in building a person in Christ, then the role of the paraclete becomes the essential second step by which we actually draw near to one another. Discipling is never a one-way channel by which we impart Christian knowledge or experience "down" to a somewhat less endowed person. Rather, discipleship is a deeply mutual experience in which two people build each other in Christ according to the proverb, "As iron sharpens iron, so one man sharpens another" (Prov. 27:17 NIV).

Years later when Wayne was living in a different community, Ann Marie and I faced an extremely distressing problem. Wayne sent a note in the mail every single day for one hundred and fifty three days! What an encouragement! I encourage you to identify those whom God has sent into your life as paracletes and to express gratitude to God for them and to those people themselves—do it by phone, by letter—that they are among the most precious, precious gifts that God has given you.

Let me also ask you to consider those for whom you are to be a paraclete. Who are those people whom God is sending you alongside to help—people who need love or encouragement or support? Sometimes we hear the marvelous expression, "standing with." A friend of mine recently shared that his wife "stood with" him during a crisis he faced. Standing with is to be a paraclete. It is to give yourself to being with—heart to heart—not merely in idle presence but actively seeking to build and to be built by one another.

Discussion Questions

1. Who has been a paraclete in your life? Recall an experience in which he or she came alongside to help you. What was the situation? How were you helped?

2. Name two people to whom God may be sending you to be a paraclete. What are their needs? How might you come alongside them? How could you help?

Chapter 4

THE WITH-ME PRINCIPLE

The concept of with-ness is far more than a description of God and people being together. It is also a prescription—a principle by which one can consciously build relationships. The community of faith says, "Come be with us." The person of faith says, "Come be with me." As Ken Medema says,

"Come with me, walk with me, run with me, fly with me. We will roam the Father's land together."[1]

The concept of the with-me principle as I know it was first expressed by Dick Halverson, the chaplain of the U.S. Senate. When some of us asked Dick when this concept first came to him, he said it was while meditating on this short verse from Mark: "And He [Jesus] appointed twelve, that they might be with Him, and that He might send them out to preach" (Mark 3:14). In this simple statement we find some of the most profound meanings inherent in the concept of "with." It was the very lifestyle of Jesus Christ to have people around Him. He chose the Twelve to be next to Him. He was constantly saying, "Follow me—come be with me." In Luke 6:40 we find the statement from Jesus Christ concerning discipleship: "A pupil is not above his teacher; but everyone, after he has been fully trained, will be like his teacher." This is the very heartbeat of Christian discipleship. To be a disciple is to be a learner, it is to be one who follows and learns from a master. There are no exceptions. If we are to grow in our own Christian discipleship, we must model Jesus Christ and become like Him by virtue of the transforming work of His Spirit. As Jesus asked people to join Him

---

[1] Ken Medema, "Come With Me." The lyrics by Ken Medema, © copyright 1973 by Word Music (a division of Word, Inc.). All rights reserved. International copyright secured. Used by permission.

at His invitation, so, too, we may have people with us at our invitation.

At least three things happened as Jesus Christ practiced this concept as stated in Mark 3:14. First, He asked people with Him simply to get to know Him as friends. We find this stated so clearly in John 15:15, "But I have called you friends." Second, He wanted them with Him so they could become like Him as His disciples. Third, He called them apostles, which means "sent ones." He invited them to be with Him so He could send them out to preach.

Discipleship, friendship, and apostleship are the three major goals of the with-me principle. Jesus Christ still practices this principle! He wants us with Him that we might get to know Him and grow through a personal friendship with Him. He wants us to become like Him. He wants to send us to lead others to Him.

Just as Jesus Christ used the with-me principle to enable people to grow as His disciples, friends, and apostles so we may use the same principle today. The with-me principle suggests that we intentionally include people in our own lives even as Jesus Christ included people in His life. As disciples of Jesus Christ we seek to live our lives the way He lives His life and to use the principles He uses. When I use the with-me principle, I want to grow in personal friendship, help that friend to become a disciple of Jesus Christ, and enable that person to become an apostle, one who is "sent to be with" other people to help them grow as disciples, friends, and apostles. In the with-me experience we grow as friends, we learn from one another with the goal of learning from Jesus Christ, and we send one another to ministry.

When Jesus Christ thinks of us, one of His first thoughts is of becoming our friend. Isn't that a wonderful idea! He delights in becoming friends with us—not simply in using us to do a work on His behalf. As you practice the with-me principle with others, remember that friendship is the primary purpose of being together. It is very easy to view time with people strictly as a means of building them as disciples of Christ. "Time with" becomes "time to teach." "Time with" becomes time to enable, to equip and to send. These are, in fact, significant reasons for "being with"—but they are not all there is. Being together in order to be friends is essential to life. Jesus modeled it and we must do it. When we grasp the utility of the with-me principle, we run the risk of using it as a means to another end: we become task oriented and people really become things, our goal being to help them become something, to do something, to uphold some agenda in life we have for them. There is an appropriate place for this task orientation, but we don't dare lose sight of Jesus Christ's concern to build friendships. We share time with people and with our Lord just to enjoy each other's presence and not just to do something together.

Of course, Jesus Christ has more in mind than just personal friendship with us and among us. Jesus asked of His Father that those who believe in Him, "be with Me where I am, in order that they may behold My glory" (John 17:24). We are with Him as friends. We are also with Him as disciples to see His glory and to worship Him, the Lord of Lords and the King of Kings. Worship and fellowship are the great ends of being with Jesus Christ. He desires that we become His friends and disciples who know, learn from, and worship Him. Then, as "apostles," we are to be sent to help other people become friends, disciples, and apostles.

Now how did Jesus Christ help people grow as friends and disciples? He grew in friendship as He shared life experiences and shared personal things with a few people. For example, when He was in the home of Mary and Martha, when he was on the Mount of Transfiguration, when He was in the Garden of Gethsemane, Jesus Christ was sharing life experiences with others and was sharing with those people the most intimate aspects of His personal life. The result was deep personal friendships.

Jesus enabled people to grow as His disciples by sharing spiritual things. In His public teachings and in His private conversations with His disciples, Jesus worked to impart spiritual insight concerning Who He was, why He came, and how they were to respond. We ourselves will grow spiritually and help others grow as disciples as well when we, too, impart spiritual things to one another.

In 1971 I was a graduate student of engineering at Purdue University. I became friends with a person named Mike Foster. Mike and I lived on the same floor of the graduate residence hall at Purdue, frequently eating together and sharing many details of life. Sharing life experiences and personal things led us to grow as personal friends. About six months into the school year Mike became very excited about the Christian faith. I attended church, but had little real concept of who Jesus Christ was. Somehow I had the idea He had come to earth to tell us about God, but that it was up to us to have our own relationship with God. Mike and I entered into long discussions in our dorm rooms. He explained how Jesus Christ is the Son of God, how He came to offer the promise of an abundant fruitful life, how His death on the cross was to eliminate the barrier that my own sin placed between me and God, and that the key to a relationship with God was faith in Jesus Christ. At first I resisted having my own beliefs about the relationship between God and Jesus Christ and people, but eventually, as I read the New Testament and was encouraged by Mike, I opened my life to Jesus Christ and began the exciting adventure that begins through personal faith in Christ. Mike helped me grow spiritually by asking me to be with him and by sharing spiritual things with me. Just as Jesus Christ helped His disciples to grow, so we can help others grow spiritually, and grow ourselves when we are willing to open our mouths and speak of the things of God.

Presence

When we are together, we are present to one another and aware of one another's presence. Presence is not necessarily saying something or doing something, but simply enjoying life in the company of one another. The ministry of presence is one of the great ways to build life through relationships. We may show presence by being physically near another person, by writing or phoning, or offering any gesture that says, "I am with you."

Dick Halverson directed me to the significance of presence when describing how, upon the occasion of a severe heart attack, he spent day after day, night after night, alone in a hospital room. When his wife, Doris, visited during the day, it was her presence that encouraged him. She was his paraclete, his helper. It wasn't what she said or what she did, though these were of significant help. It was simply who she was and where she was—near him—that counted. And when Doris left, Dick felt the most intense sense of loss, of despair, of a desire to have her again by his side. Presence suggests that we come to need one another not only because of what will be said or what will be done but because we love one another. We want to be near each other.

Because I live in the Midwest, I am not often able to have fellowship with my brother Jim who lives in Los Angeles. Intensely interested in the worldwide missionary movement, after Christmas one year Jim attended the Urbana Missionary Conference sponsored by the Intervarsity Christian Fellowship. That conference was only two hours from our home, so Jim drove over one Sunday afternoon to visit. We spent four hours laughing and joking, and finally the time came for us to part. He wanted to get something at the church on his way out of town, so he followed me in his car as I led him over to the church. Staring at his face in the rear view mirror as we drove along, I was suddenly overwhelmed with the depth of my love for him and with great sorrow that soon our cars would go in different directions. It wasn't his words I knew I would miss or his actions, though both are a joy, but his presence. When God gives us friendships within our family and with others within the church and in other places, He is allowing us to experience the rich privilege of shared presence.

When we meet someone for the first time there are often the awkward moments in which we fumble for things to talk about—common experiences or ideas that we might share. We fish for topics of conversation that will allow us to get to know one another. As we share in life experiences by actually doing things together, and as we begin to share personal things, our relationship grows into authentic friendship. We find peace in simply being near the other person. Silence becomes comfortable in the knowledge that nothing needs to be said. We don't have to say something or do something to justify ourselves to the other person.

My friend Bill Fall closes his prayers with the

words, "Help us to practice the presence of God." What a marvelous discipline that is. As we consciously and constantly seek to be aware of God's presence, we can know the moment-by-moment joy of being with the Spirit of God. His is the great Presence, and He extends the great ministry of presence to us all that we may delight in Him.

Discussion Questions

1. Can you describe an occasion upon which someone else used the with-me principle on you and invited you to join him? What happened?
2. What excites you about the with-me principle?
3. What concerns you about the with-me principle?
4. Recall an incident when you appreciated the simple presence of someone else.
5. Share an event in which you were keenly aware of the presence of God.

Chapter 5

PUTTING WITH-ME TO WORK

Jesus Christ used the with-me principle as an intentional way of building friendships, growing disciples, and sending them out as apostles to make disciples of others. The concept of the with-me principle adds an exciting dimension to the Christian life because we realize that in every human encounter, every time we are "with" another person or with a group there is a unique opportunity for God to do something with our lives. Now how do we practice this principle today? How do we actually involve people with us in life that we may grow as friends and grow spiritually as well? Essential to our practice is the ministry of invitation.

Invitation means that I take the initiative to include other persons in my life or even to seek to include my life in theirs. So I invite those persons to "Come with me. Join me. Be a part of this group with me. Come to my home for a meal. Let's go to that movie together. Let's share in that retreat together. Or may I help you [be with you] as you dig your garden? May I join you in painting that room? May I be a part of the group you're in?"

Most of the people you associate with are people you have probably met in a group or an activity that someone else is sponsoring and who have come on their own initiative, not yours. Just as Jesus Christ had people with Him by His invitation, so we, too, need to involve people in our own lives through our invitation. Of course, waiting for someone else to ask us to participate in some event or activity or to join them for a meal is certainly an acceptable aspect of every person's life. There are times when appropriately, we want others to take the initiative to invite us. However, to use the with-me principle we must also take the initiative. We must be saying, "Lord, who do you want with me? How can we be involved in one another's lives?"

Initiative means taking the next step. Initiative is action. Initiative is movement. To take no initiative with other people is to be a sheep, is to be one of the flock. To take initiative is to become a shepherd. It's to reach out. It's to make "being with" an intentional act. Think about the people with whom you associate on a regular basis. Ask, "Are we together on my initiative or theirs?"

You might be inclined to think that the concept of asking people to join you upon your invitation requires a certain kind of outgoing personality. I know of a person who practices this principle every day and yet has probably never heard of it as such. He simply has a winsome, outgoing spirit that draws people to him, and wherever he goes he has people around him. I don't believe I have ever seen him alone. He is a natural practicer of this principle. Yet if Jesus Christ practices a principle and I am to become like Him, then I must practice it, too. In that sense, the with-me principle has nothing to do with personality. It has to do with my initiative and willingness to invite. I don't consider myself a particularly outgoing person, and yet I have found that by taking initiative and inviting people to join me in whatever I happen to be doing, the principle can be easily used. God has used it over and over again to give me new friends, to help me grow in Christ, and to help them grow in Christ as well.

The ministry of invitation does require courage. For me to initiate in another person's life can be a little scary. It's as though there is a little wall between me and the other person—an emotional wall. My own emotions, my own fears become a barrier between us. If I am not willing to leap that little wall and to invite, then with-me is dead. I may still be in groups among other people, but the concept of building life on purpose, of intentionally involving people in my life according to my style, according to my personality, nevertheless demands that I "leap the wall" and take action.

One of our favorite activities as a family is to go to a local Baskin-Robbins for ice cream. We used to just pile in the car and go as a family. As the idea of invitation grew, we began to ask other families to go. I "leap the wall" and make two or three phone calls and eventually find some family that is delighted to go. We drive to the store together, eat ice cream with kids running everywhere, and grow in friendship through this shared life experience.

Recently I wanted to ask three other men to meet with me for a four-week Bible study as an encouragement to our growth in Christ. Every one is an extremely busy, successful businessman. I had to "leap the wall," take initiative by picking up the phone and inviting them. All three said "yes" and we had a terrific series of meetings. With-me means I leap over my own fear of inviting others and ask them to join me in fellowship, ministry, life, and leisure. As we are together, God enables us to build each other as personal friends with one another and as disciples of Jesus Christ.

Positioning

The practice of the with-me principle for growing in friendships and discipleship expands considerably when we consider the different ways we come to be with people. I have described the concept of using personal invitation to include people with us in our own lives or seeking to be with them in their lives. Yet God on His own initiative places us among a great many people in life with whom we have the opportunity to grow in friendship, discipleship, and apostleship.

When my friend Mike Foster asked me if I had ever given my life to Jesus Christ, that question led to a whole series of discussions through which I was led to a serious commitment to Jesus Christ. Later in the summer of 1972, I was a college student attending the great gathering of Christian youth in Dallas, Texas, known as Explo '72. I was listening to a lecture on youth ministry when some people entered the room and sat down next to me. I realized that I had met the woman who sat beside me, although I did not know her well. She was from my town in Indiana! In two years Ann Marie and I were married!

Were those two encounters just coincidences? Or was God's hand directly involved in bringing Ann Marie and me together and in leading Mike and me together? All of us can recount experience after experience in which we recognize the hand of God positioning us with people.

I am convinced that God positions us next to the people of His choice. He puts us with people in order that we might build each other and accomplish His purposes. Think back to the significant events of your life and I'm sure that you will remember several moments in which you can see God's hand positioning key people in your life.

The concept of positioning can be clearly seen in the book of Acts. It is amazing to see how the lives of those early Christians crossed one another and how much ministry resulted—such as the meeting of Paul and Barnabas or the meeting of Paul and Timothy or the meeting of Paul and the Philippian jailer.

I shared the idea of positioning with our congregation a few years ago and was astonished at how quickly it became a part of our daily vocabulary ("yesterday God positioned me with a person who . . ."). People recognize that God is at work in their lives and that He has a hand in positioning them with people. The concept of positioning helps us to have the eyes to see God at work in our daily encounters with other people. God puts us next to others that we may become friends and minister to each other.

Some time ago I was sitting in our car with our two children while Ann Marie, my wife, was shopping. During that time two friends walked up to my window to chat. We enjoyed a brief but terrific time of fellowship and each went on his way. Three hours later I suddenly realized, "Oh, yeah! I had been praying specifically for those two men." God positioned us in that parking lot so that we could encourage each other. I knew it was no accident. That meeting was something that Jesus Christ arranged in order to build our friendship. God positions people.

Gene Loomis is a man with whom I am interested in developing a personal relationship so that we can encourage each other in the Christian faith and grow as friends. When I arrived at the library to write these pages, I found this same man whose office is many miles away also entering the library. He had come to prepare a speech. Was it an accident that we both arrived at the library at the same moment? No! God chooses to arrange the parts of the Body of Christ in such a way that we may build one another and fulfill His purposes.

The Christian life really becomes exciting when God gives us the eyes to see Him at work, when He gives us the eyes to see an event of daily life and to realize, "Wow! God was involved in that event in some way. He wants to bring something good out of it." The concept of positioning suggests that we can see God at work in our very being together with people, and that we can expect Him to work when we are together. Expecting God to work in our daily relationships is a marvelous way to see that God is a God of our daily life, interested in our moment-by-moment experiences.

The Bible is the record of God at work through events that He has envisioned people to see. In the Old Testament we have the mighty acts of the Exodus and the parting of the Red Sea. In the New Testament we see the works of Jesus Christ and His resurrection. God didn't stop his work two thousand years ago. He is as active and vibrant a God today as ever. All we need is the power of sight to perceive

Him working and positioning people with people, and oh, the excitement that gives to us as Christian people today!

Now, there is a mystery to the concept of positioning. "The mind of man plans his way, But the LORD directs his steps" (Prov. 16:9). Although Jesus Christ, the Head, positions me as a member of His Body, I also position myself! I am the one who decided to attend Explo '72 and that particular youth seminar where I met my future wife. I am the one who decided to attend Purdue University where I was introduced to Jesus Christ. There was no postcard in the mail that said, "Memo to Stanley Ott from God: 'Position yourself in Dallas in 1972 or go to Purdue.'" Yet, it is clear that in the grace of God, those events were no accident for me. He repeatedly positions us with people to fulfill a purpose that will "work together for good" (Rom. 8:28).

Francis Schaeffer has observed that God is sovereign and we are significant. Both are crucial to a biblical view. On the one hand, we recognize that God is sovereign. It means that He is the one who positions us, HE is in charge. On the other hand, we are significant. God does lead us, and our decisions do have true meaning.

Occasionally we will find ourselves positioned with a person who is either hurting or hurtful. We must remember that God is not the author of evil, but uses evil for good. He uses all things to fulfill His intent to love us and to build us in the image of His Son. When we find ourselves positioned with a hurting or hurtful person, we must go to God, the faithful God, the God of power, and trust Him to help us relate to that person appropriately.

The concept of positioning suggests two rather practical ways we may live our lives before the face of God. The first is very simple: See God at work whenever you are with another person. Trust Him to build your friendship with that person and to fulfill His purpose with the two of you. Pray, "Lord, how can we grow as friends and how can we help each other grow spiritually?"

Second, to borrow a sports term, we "play the position." Mark Hermann is a former all-American quarterback from Purdue University who was a legitimate candidate for the Heisman Trophy, the highest award in college football. Why? Because he played his position well!

Every time we are with another person we have a choice to play the position—to grow as friends and to minister to that person. In the idea of positioning we have the image of being sent, that is, sent by God to be with that person. Therefore, we should never let the opportunity for friendship or ministry pass by. When God positions you with someone in your family, in your neighborhood, at work, or in the church, begin to pray silently. Ask God, "How can we grow as friends? How can I invite this person to be with me so that we may grow as friends, and if possible, as disciples of Christ?"

Discussion Questions

1. What does initiative mean?
2. Describe two or three things you do in your life in which you could invite someone else to be with you.
3. Try to recall an event in which you can see the hand of God positioning you and another person together.
4. How are the concepts of the with-me principle and positioning related?

Chapter 6

FRIEND WITH
FRIEND

Soon after I had stepped into the excitement of the Christian faith, a good friend of mine, Stanley Ide, and I met at the "Sweet Shop," a great snack bar meeting place for students on the Purdue University campus. After we had talked for a while about life in general, to my surprise, Stanley pulled out a Bible and said, "Stan, let me share a passage of Scripture with you that is really challenging me." He opened to Daniel 4, and we read

together how God humbled the great king Nebu-
chadnezzar. Now Stanley was simply sharing with
me the thing that was exciting him spiritually, but
wow—what an impact that made on my life! God
used that moment to really challenge me with the
concept that He is truly the King and I am His
servant. In sharing spiritual things with me, Stanley
furthered our own personal friendship and built me
as a disciple of Jesus Christ.

Friendship is in trouble today. Fast paced life,
rising divorce rates, increasing numbers of people
dependent on drugs—all indicate that somehow the
fabric of relationships in our society is being pulled
apart. In a sense we live in "an isolated society,"
which is really a contradiction in terms, because
"society" suggests being with or being together and
"isolated" suggests being apart. Just think of the
factors that have entered life in this generation that
tend to isolate person from person and to reduce the
number of personal friendships. Shopping malls
have ended friendships with shop owners because
it's possible to shop by phone, bank by phone, and
work by phone. Air-conditioning not only keeps
houses cool, it keeps people inside. Television leads
families to stare at a wall rather than to talk to each
other. From my back porch on a typical summer day
I can see fifteen suburban houses without a single
adult outside.

It is increasingly true that if you want friends,
you will have to use the with-me principle—to use
the ministry of invitation to include people in your

life, in events, and in ways that will allow a bond of love to develop between you.

In thinking about friendship, I like to make the distinction between friends of the road and friends of the heart that Jane Howard makes.[1] She discusses the different kinds of friends that were originally reported by Robert Brain in his study of the Bangwa African tribe.[2] A friend of the road is a person with whom you grow in friendship because you are walking life's road together. You may be living in the same neighborhood, working in the same office, have children in the same school, or participate in the same church. As you walk life's road together, you have the opportunity to develop a true friendship. You grow in love for one another, share personal concerns, and offer encouragement and companionship. A friend-of-the-road relationship, however, is a temporary friendship in that it only lasts while you walk the same road. Should you leave your workplace or move to another community or change churches, those friendships of the road come to an end. Of course, were you to rejoin such a friend, the friendship could quickly rekindle. There is nothing wrong with a friendship of the road. It is genuine enough, but simply temporary, and lasts only while you are together.

[1]Jane Howard, *Families*, (New York: Simon and Schuster, 1978), 283.

[2]Robert Brain, *Friends and Lovers* (London: Hart-Davis, MacGibbon, Ltd., 1976), 108.

On the other hand, a friend of the heart is a deep, permanent, longlasting relationship. Somehow, in the friend of the heart, we find a person to whom our soul is knit even as Jonathan and David's souls were knit together in love. A friendship of the heart is a relationship we maintain and treasure whether we are in the same place or whether one of us moves to the other side of the world. When we're together, it's difficult to distinguish between friends of the road and friends of the heart, because both represent true friendships we have in some life situation. But when we separate, the true friend of the heart surfaces because we realize this is a lifetime relationship that God has given us. Of course, the majority of our friends are friends of the road—given us by God that we may share a portion of life together. As we walk life's road "with" people, we develop friendships, and rejoice whenever God moves one off the road and into the heart.

When the apostle Paul wrote his friend Philemon about Onesimus, he said, "I have sent him [Onesimus] back to you in person, that is, sending my very heart." For a person to become "my very heart" is to suggest that we share life at the deepest levels, that we are "with" one another in the sense of the New Testament Greek word *"sun."* For *"sun,"* as we have noted, is more than being with each other on a casual acquaintance level. Rather, it comes to mean the sharing of all of life. It is *koinonia.* It is committing myself and my possessions and my life and my time to you even as you commit yours to me.

With-me in friendship suggests that as we share a road with others, we take the initiative to invite people to be with us that we might grow in our relationship with them, and we ask God to give us friendships of the heart.

There are a number of ways in which we can build friendships, both friendships of the road and friendships that move off the road and into the heart. The essence of every approach to building friendship is to maintain the concept of with-ness as we include people in our lives, and as we learn to include the person of Jesus Christ in our friendship.

We build depth in friendship as we spend significant time "with" a few people, sharing in life's experiences and sharing personal things. Jesus Christ spent a significant time among the Twelve. In fact, Judas knew where to find Him at the time of the betrayal, as Jesus often met in the Garden of Gethsemane with His disciples (John 18:2). They shared life experiences as they shared personal things: their hopes, dreams, fears, and plans. We grow in friendship as we, too, share personal things with each other. Why do so many college roommates become friends of the heart? Because they experience so much together and have shared so many of their hopes, dreams, and fears.

One of the greatest ways I know to grow friendships is to get into a small group Bible study for the purpose of study, sharing of personal blessings and needs, and prayer together. This is what Jesus did with the Twelve. As people meet week in and week out, sharing personal and spiritual things, incredible bonds of friendship will develop among them where there may have originally been very little "chemistry" among them.

Of course, Jesus' disciples were with Him in many of life's experiences other than small group study and prayer. For example, they were with Him at the marriage in Cana of Galilee. They ate together at the home of Mary, Martha, and Lazarus. They shared life, leisure, and ministry together. As you include people in your life, leisure, and ministry (whether you're painting your house or going to some sports event or a Christian fellowship), you are creating the opportunity to build friendships of the road and of the heart. We employ the with-me principle as we use the ministry of invitation to involve people with us in our life experiences in which we share personal things.

A second significant way to develop a friendship of the heart is to share spiritual things with your friends. Jesus Christ shared many spiritual things with those closest to Him. The very things that help people grow spiritually will bind them together as friends. Again we see the effectiveness of the small group Bible study not only in building friends but in discipling, for in that group we share personal and spiritual things. However, in our many encounters with people outside of a small group, we will have natural opportunities to speak of spiritual things.

One of the greatest ways to share spiritual things with another person is by praying with that person on a regular basis. That's one way a small group Bible study can build friendship; yet this is a concept you can use with just one or two other people. As I think about the closest friends I have had in my life, I realize that with most of them I have spent time in prayer, meeting once a week, once a month, or simply praying casually during time together. We pray for the needs we sense in each other's lives. We pray for the needs of others we see. Somehow when two people pray together, it knits them together at the deepest possible levels.

Discussing spiritual things certainly can go beyond prayer. In fact, you may have friendships in which prayer between you seems a bit inappropriate at the time, but freedom to discuss spiritual things is there. Rich Boonstra and Karl Zilm were two men with whom I had the privilege of attending Purdue over a two-year period. Since we shared our meals and our social lives together, we became very close friends of the road. I remember after knowing one another for a year, sitting one evening in Karl's dorm room. I was on his bed—Karl and Rich were on chairs. I was excited about my new faith in Jesus Christ, and hesitantly but deliberately brought up the subject of the Christian faith. I had no idea where those men were in their spiritual life even though we had been friends for over a year.

Then I discovered that Karl, a Lutheran, and Rich, Christian Reformed, were lifelong members of their churches. Both were much more mature Christians than I, and a whole new avenue of conversation and relationship opened for us. Our friendships began to move off the road and into the heart.

Now, do you think it is appropriate to bring up personal and spiritual things every time you are with someone? Of course not! Many of our associations with people don't offer an appropriate avenue to speak of deeper things. Yet, as you share in life experiences with others, you will have all kinds of very good opportunities to talk about the personal and spiritual dimensions of life.

It is so easy for us to have a close friend, and for some reason (perhaps because we are so familiar with one another or we're simply afraid of rejection), one of us fails to bring up the spiritual dimension of our lives. Yet, this is one dimension that will move our relationship into the heart. Often it takes courage to speak about spiritual matters with a friend, not for the purpose of forcing our conversations on that friend, but rather to share spiritual as well as common social concerns. To have the freedom and the courage to share with a friend what God is doing in your life means that you are "with" your friend socially and spiritually. As John makes clear in his first epistle, fellowship is "with" the Father and His Son Jesus Christ, and it is "with" one another. In speaking of spiritual things with our friends, we are sharing in intimate fellowship with them.

Discussion Questions

1. What are some of the factors in your life that may prevent you from developing new friendships?

2. Think about some of your current friends. Are they friends of the road or of the heart?

3. What are the ways this chapter suggests you can build deeper friendships?

4. What specifically will you do with one current friend or a potential friend to help your relationship grow?

Chapter 7

BUILDING YOUR FAMILY RHYTHMS

I have more fun using the with-me principle in my family than in any other place. The idea of family could almost be defined by the concept of "with." When I first thought of using this principle at home, it occurred to me that I went on a number of trips to stores alone on which I could have included one or more children. Consciously, I remember saying to Lee one day, "I'm going to the drug store, Lee, do you want to go with me?"

"Sure, Dad," he said excitedly. As we drove to the store he said, "Dad, do worms yawn?!" Now that wasn't exactly a statement of great spiritual insight, but I must admit, it's something I'll treasure all my life.

On another occasion I took Lee with me on Halloween while running an errand. Lee was five, about the age at which children begin to think about the concept that God is everywhere. Lee said to me, "Dad, is it true that God is everywhere?"

"Yes, son, God is everywhere!"

"Well, Dad, would God be in a pumpkin?"

I wasn't exactly sure how to handle that question but the logic of the whole thing led me to say, "Yes."

"Well, Dad, WHY would God want to be in a pumpkin?"

He had me!

One Saturday I was preparing to attend a college retreat for which I was responsible, and it occurred to me to take Lee along as an expression of the with-me principle. It was only after the idea came to me that I realized how sensible it was, because at the retreat there would be a hundred built-in baby-sitters!

As we drove toward the retreat center, we were talking about Indians and bows and arrows when suddenly Lee asked what the retreat was about. I explained that college students were meeting to learn how to be friends of Jesus. Lee asked, "Dad, can I be a friend of Jesus, too?" During that conversation and a little time of prayer in the car, Lee made his very first commitment to Jesus Christ. With-me in my family simply means that when I'm doing something, I try to include someone from my family.

It used to be my custom to have my devotional Quiet Time early in the morning—alone downstairs in the den. I would shut the door, and as a child approached I would send the youngster away saying, "Leave me alone. I'm having a prayer time with the Lord." I was talking about Quiet Time one day with a good friend Dick Feiertag who said, "Stan, you're missing one of the greatest modeling opportunities your children will ever have. Instead of sending them away during your Quiet Time, why don't you allow them to join you?"

Dick was actually telling me to use the with-me principle in my Quiet Time! So I told the children when they came to the den that I was praying, and if they wanted to join me in prayer they were welcome, but if not, I would join them later upstairs.

One morning, three-year-old Lindsay joined me. After explaining that she could stay and pray or leave, she chose to stay, and climbed onto my lap. I began to pray for Mommy and for Lee and for Lindsay when it occurred to me to pray that Lindsay's friends might one day come to know Jesus as their friend. So we said, "Lord, we pray that Janice will know Jesus as her friend and Ellen will know Jesus as her friend . . ." and before I could think of another child's name, Lindsay said, "and Lindsay."

So I said, "Does Lindsay want Jesus to be her friend?"

She answered, "Yes, Daddy."

I explained that all she had to do was ask Him to come into her life and He would be her friend always. We prayed together. Now, years later, she still remembers that experience and knows clearly that she asked Christ into her life. If I had not been practicing the with-me principle with my family, I would have missed those two most precious opportunities.

Just as the with-me principle was used by Jesus to help people grow as friends and as disciples and ultimately as apostles, so the with-me principle has the same function in my family. You see, at the very heart of discipleship is the concept that we are growing closer to Jesus Christ, and that we are doing it with others.

The joy of discipling in our own family is that we have the privilege of drawing closer to Jesus Christ together, and at the same time, of discovering fresh levels of love and friendship among ourselves. Taking the initiative to be with members of our family gives us opportunity to share in personal and spiritual things—to grow as friends as we share in life's experiences, whether driving to the drug store or going to a college retreat. As a result we grow in relationship. We grow as disciples. The family becomes the source of strength from which we are sent to ministry as "apostles" into our various worlds.

The very pressures and aspects of our society

that make developing personal friendship difficult also press against the quality of family life. It is essential to ask the question, "How can I build with-ness into my family's life?" As we share in the wide range of life's experiences, are there concerns and hurts I am experiencing that I need to be sharing? Are there joys and blessings that I need to be sharing as well?

Although I use the with-me principle to include family members in things I am doing, I am also concerned with the overall togetherness of the family. We want to develop the sense of family that comes as we help all the relationships in the family to grow.

Rhythm

I believe an essential concept to grasp in building family friendships is the concept of rhythm. Rhythm suggests that there is a beat, a cadence, a regular movement or cycle to life. Our normal life rhythm includes three meals a day, seven nights of sleep a week, work during the weekdays, and church on Sunday. Our culture has become increasingly busy and frenetic as people are offered a greater variety of activities in which to participate, all of which are good in themselves. I frequently talk to people who are overly committed as they go from work to meeting, from home to church, to an entertainment event, to a social event, to a sport event, and to another meeting. Instead of having a sense of being paced and unhurried, life becomes almost over-whelming in its press and variety.

We can lean against the culture as we deliber-ately establish with-ness rhythms in our personal life and in the life of our family. For example, the devotional Quiet Time I spend each day with God is the result of a deliberate rhythm I have placed in my life so that I may be "with" God. Let me suggest six rhythms that you may build into your family's life: the couple's night out, the child's meal out, the escape weekend, the escape weekend for the family, the family table, and the blessing cup. Every rhythm offers an opportunity to share life's experiences, personal things, and spiritual things. Every rhythm is a with-me opportunity to grow in friendship and discipleship through the ministry of invitation.

Perhaps the most useful rhythm for marriage and family life is the meal out. When Ann Marie and I were about to be married, our friend Dave Van Zandt sent us an article by Charlie Shedd that described the pattern by which he and Martha went out for a meal every single week. At first I balked at the idea. Quick calculation suggested such a routine would practically cost the price of a new house over forty years of marriage! But when Ann Marie and I actually had the privilege of hearing the Shedds talk in person about their getaway times, we decided to do it. We have never regretted the decision. No matter how demanding and turbulent the schedule of life becomes, we stick to our night out every Monday evening.

There are usually two subjects of conversation when we go out. The first is simply to "debrief" and recount the events of the day. We cover some of the basic things that every couple needs to review, and share some of the blessings we are experiencing. Then I like to ask Ann Marie, "What is your 'angst' (your deepest anxiety, where you are concerned, where you are at this moment)?" We try to connect with each other at a slightly deeper level than we do in the ordinary conversation. For some reason, we find that the setting of a restaurant really assists this time of sharing. There is something about being at a restaurant table that makes it easier to share things of more meaning and depth. This has been even more true during our young-children phase of life. At home everyone wants to talk at once. We practically need a referee. We've found that a night out, week in and week out, over the years has given us a way of touching bases and maintaining a rapport that nothing else provides.

I suggest if you are single that this practice is still valid—have a regular meal out with a close friend. Sharing your lives and encouraging one another will provide the greatest possible support for you. There is something about a meal that heightens the depth of an interpersonal experience. Breaking bread together, lingering at the table, and sharing one's life can lead one to form the deepest bonds of life with another.

The Shedds extend out to children the idea of eating a shared meal. Following their pattern, I have taken each of our children out to lunch alone once every month, beginning around their second birthday. I am amazed at the depth of conversation during these lunches, and love the fun of a special time with each child. At first I had to remember to take each child out every month. As they have grown older, they remind me! Ann Marie also takes the children out alone for a meal. It is a great rhythm for building communication.

A third rhythm we have found useful for our marriage once or twice a year is the concept of the escape weekend. Actually we're usually gone for only twenty-four hours but when carefully planned, that time provides a tremendous opportunity for sharing and intimacy at levels we cannot achieve during the meal out or at home during the normal course of life. When children are involved, we make certain to hire a competent baby-sitter so that the care of our children will not be a concern. We have found a basic six-step sequence that works well for us, but that certainly could be adapted or altered a thousand ways.

First, we like to travel for about an hour away from home because that gives us time to wind down and log in with each other. Further, it means we are easily accessible if we should need to return home. Second, we like to go to a nice restaurant—a place where the service will be excellent and where we can remain and talk for a long time.

Third, we like to focus the conversation during that meal on the previous six months to a year. We share where we have seen God's blessings at work during those months and our current "angsts"—that is, where we are at this moment, both in terms of blessings and personal need. We return to the motel for a romantic night. Fifth, we like a leisurely breakfast. Usually a motel will have a kind of dining room where we can linger and talk after the meal. We try to focus the conversation on the future. We discuss what we need to be doing in our family's life and in our personal and professional lives for the next six months to a year. Sixth, and finally, we return home. Sometimes we work some shopping in after breakfast, but usually we are home within twenty-four hours. We are amazed at how much energy we receive from those weekends. It is a tremendous time for renewing our personal love and friendship and for getting in touch with God *together*.

A fourth rhythm simply extends the marriage escape weekend to the whole family. Once or twice a year we take the family to a motel with a pool where we can spend a day or two together just playing and having fun. Those times provide intense moments of family joy and they produce great memories.

A fifth rhythm we find very helpful is the concept of a family table. Every Sunday night after supper the family has the "family table." First we share blessings we have received during the last week with a specific awareness that God has provided those blessings. With young children, of course, the nature of the blessing they share may be seemingly trivial, but in the total flow of a family's life we gain a sense that all blessings are from God. After sharing blessings, we move to a time of sharing personal concerns, especially concerns we have with respect to our family life and each other. Sometimes one child has a complaint against another, sometimes we have to discuss the issue of picking up the house or improving our spirits with one another. Whatever the concerns may be, the family table is an accepted place to share such needs without any spirit of implied criticism. It's a time for us to talk about those things and come to some kind of resolution. After our sharing, we then pray aloud conversationally, thanking God for the blessings and asking for His help with the concerns.

A final rhythm we find most helpful is the concept of the "blessing cup." We were introduced to this idea through a booklet by Rock Travnikar.[1] As we use it, the blessing cup provides a way for highlighting very special events in the life of the family and recognizing them as blessings from God. We have a cup that is set aside solely for use by the family as the blessing cup. When not in use, it is in some prominent place in the dining room. On the occasion of a special day such as Easter, Christmas, or a special event in the life of someone in the family (such as a child's first success in riding a bicycle or graduation from school or a birthday), we pour into the cup any liquid that everyone is willing to drink

---

[1] Rock Travnikar, O. F. M., *The Blessing Cup* (Cincinnati: St. Anthony Messenger Press, 1979).

(ours is apple juice!) and place it on the table during the regular evening meal. After the meal, we pass the cup, sharing one blessing about the day, "I am thankful for Easter because . . ." or "I am thankful for Shelley because . . ." Then the person offering the blessing takes a sip. If someone is being honored, that one is the last to receive the cup and to say something and to drink from the cup. All of us then have a moment of prayer thanking God aloud for the special day or the special person. We've discovered over the months and years that the cup comes to have high significance. It represents the blessings of God, and is a way for us to affirm and build up one another.

Each of these rhythms has been useful to us in helping our marriage and family grow together. Every one of these rhythms can be altered a hundred ways, and there are many other rhythms, too, that a family can build into its schedule. At stake is some kind of regular way by which the family can guarantee time together to affirm God's blessings and each other, and to *do* it no matter how harried, busy or demanding life may be. In a world that tends to isolate people from each other, we want consciously to build into life rhythms that will develop relationships. These rhythms form the basis of what it means for us to be a family and to grow in Christ together.[2]

Discussion Questions

1. How can you use the with-me principle to develop your relationship with each member of your family?

2. What rhythms do you presently use to build time together into your family's life? What additional rhythms could you add?

3. Discuss one of the rhythms described in the last chapter that would advance the relationships in your family.

Chapter 8

DOING MINISTRY AT WORK

One day a friend of mine, John Stewart, was having lunch with fellow workers at his company in Pittsburgh. Halfway through lunch one of the men asked John, "What is the purpose of life?" John said, "I was so surprised I almost choked on my hoagie! I shared with him that I thought the purpose of life is serving Jesus Christ and growing to know Him and serving people." John went on to share how delighted he was that his friendship with this man was a bridge by which he could share the good news of Christ. Relationships at work are one means for sharing the Good News, and they are essential to personal friendship and a healthy work life.

Vital to each of our lives is the work we perform. It is one of our primary means of service to Jesus Christ as we work "unto Him." It's how we provide for our family and ourselves, and it is one of our most significant arenas for personal ministry. The with-me principle is certainly not limited to our church, family, or fellowship, for it is basic to Christian lifestyle and is to be used everywhere. We want to develop friendships among the people around us at work, and we want to lead them to Christ and His church when the opportunities appear. The people at your workplace have been positioned there by God that you might grow as friends and, whenever possible, build one another as followers of Jesus Christ.

Dick Feiertag used to travel two hours south of town to visit another company site, and on those trips would always take one of his subordinates. I asked Dick if he took along that subordinate in order to discuss business and Dick surprised me by saying, "No, I have only one goal and that is to build my friendship with that man so that our working relationship might be more effective."

I was talking to Bill Faith, a friend who was involved in marketing for a major chemical corporation. As he explained some of the social events that he attended on behalf of the company, he commented that a company really is nothing more than people. We tend to view a company in terms of its products or its advertising, but companies are people—people in relationships with people—and good relationships make for healthy companies.

In your workplace it's very possible to use the with-me principle to develop relationships with associates, subordinates, and with superiors—not to use them but to know them, to grow in real friendships, and when possible, to share the good news of Christ with them as well.

Every occupation offers unique with-me opportunities, moments in which you can grow in friendship, and grow spiritually as well. As you become sensitive to the concept of inviting people to join you, you will find golden opportunities (just as Dick's taking an associate with him on his out-of-town trips, and John Stewart's spending time with coworkers at lunch). Let me share some of those opportunities as they exist within different professions.

In business, a person is constantly involved in transactions. Business can be an endless succession of superficial relationships in which agreements are made and understandings given. Yet, in business you can focus on a few people within your business world with whom you would like to develop a personal, real friendship. Begin to eat lunches with them. Have them to your home. Invite them when you travel, as you attend a seminar, and as you make transactions. Include them not merely because it's good business, but because you are seeking to share life and develop real friendships with them.

The profession of pastor is typically a "lone ranger" profession. Pastors tend to prepare for sermons alone, travel to meetings alone, attend events to speak alone, and offer pastoral care alone. Obviously, some of these may have to be done alone. As a pastor, however, there are many things you do that can be done with people. Invite a few people into a small group Bible study, or have someone join you as you visit in the hospital or in a home. If you speak at an event in another church or before some civic group, take a person or two with you as driving companions. If you travel to a seminar, be certain to include some people from your church. When you conduct a funeral service, personally invite someone to accompany you to the funeral home and to the cemetery, then home. In all of these opportunities, your conversation on the way to the event will likely be typical chat about weather, sports, and other events of interest. But after the event at which you have preached or seen someone who is ill or shared the Gospel, you'll discover that the conversation on the way home is more intimate. You'll be sharing much more personal particular, and will have a tremendous opportunity to talk about spiritual things.

The university professor has an incredible opportunity to use the with-me principle. Professors with graduate students have a built-in system for including people in their lives. It is easy for professors to relate to their students strictly concerning matters of research and study requirements. Students can use the major professor solely as an advisor to check off courses taken, to guide research, and to edit a thesis. The professor who uses the graduate system as a means of intentionally including people to build those students has a tremendous opportunity. Invite a few students to join you when you teach a class, attend a seminar, or do research. Then go out for a hamburger and talk about it. Have them in your home, and invite them to your church to give them a chance to see you in all phases of life. They become a master of your subject area not just because of courses taken, but because they begin to glean something of your life interest and what you are giving your life to. Watch for the natural opportunities to discuss personal and spiritual matters that arise.

Teachers in any school system have many opportunities to include children when preparing for the next day's work or when preparing an activity for the class or a function for the school. Look for opportunities to involve students with you. Look for ways to invite other teachers and staff in your school system to join you both in professional events and in life and leisure. Use the ministry of invitation to develop personal friendships among those who share your working life with you.

Managing a home is a full-time profession for many women and it also offers an infinite number of with-me opportunities. There are opportunities to include children in your normal activities of planning, shopping, and the care of the home. There are opportunities for you and your children to share in creative activities such as art, games, or attending some event. More than any other person you have the opportunity to involve children in the with-me principle in all phases of life.

The person who stays at home often has some control over scheduling, and can plan to spend quality time with other adults. Invite people to a morning coffee, a lunch, into a home Bible study, or to a service project. Those intentional times together build your friendship and give opportunities for spiritual growth as well.

High school and college students have almost unlimited opportunities to be together. You can include people as you participate in school activities and in sports. You can include people as you attend events and as you work on projects. Notice that if you simply participate in school activities, you are not necessarily practicing the with-me principle, because those people may be there on their own initiative and the actual activity may have been initiated by the school itself. But when you, on your own initiative, invite people to join you in activities, then you are consciously using the principle to build friendships and relationships. For example, "John, I'm going to see the Space Exhibit in the gym. How about coming with me?"

No matter what your particular work may be,

there are certainly people with whom you have contact. Who are the people whom you can invite while you work, on break, during lunch, and after work as you are together at home or in various forms of recreation? As you take the initiative with those people to include them in your life, you learn to build true friendships with them, and prayerfully, and hopefully, to have an opportunity to share spiritual things with them.

In essence, we seek to build friendship and discipleship with our coworkers intentionally by taking the initiative and either inviting them to join us or by seeking to include ourselves in their lives. Our goal is real relationships—to develop friends of the heart and to be Christ's servant, sent to these people to build them in Christ and to meet their needs. Relationships at work, as in every other context of life, can be strictly casual. When we make discipling an intentional part of life, we begin to ask ourselves, "How can I build a friendship with this coworker? How can I grow in relationship with that associate? How can I move this relationship from a strictly professional basis to a personal one as well?"

Discussion Questions

1. Why use the with-me principle at your place of work?

2. What excites you and concerns you about using it at work?

3. What are opportunities to use the with-me principle at work? What opportunities do you have in
   your work day that lend themselves to including
   people in your life?

Chapter 9

DISCIPLING IN YOUR MINISTRY

Perhaps the greatest means of building people is to include them as you are involved in ministry for Jesus Christ. Jesus Himself did this in all phases of His ministry. When the five thousand people were hungry, who fed them? Jesus broke the bread and the fish, but the twelve disciples who were with Him fed them. When Jesus raised the dead son of the widow of Nain, the disciples were there. When He taught and preached and healed as recorded in Matthew 9, the disciples were with Him, and in Matthew 10 we find Jesus sending them to do that which they had seen Him do.

As I mentioned in the last chapter, people involved in ministry tend to perform their ministry alone. I tend to go to the church and teach my class alone. If there are other teachers, usually someone else recruited them. If I am an usher in my church, I probably don't usher alone, but the other ushers were not recruited by me but by someone else. If I visit in the hospital, I visit alone. If I go to speak before a group, usually I go alone and come back alone. There is a lone-ranger mentality to ministry, yet even the Lone Ranger had Tonto! Jesus Christ involved other people with Him as he built people and the crucial reality is that people don't get a heart for ministry just because we teach them. People *catch* ministry! It is a vision more caught during with-me time than taught.

Cal Markham is a friend of mine who accepted the pastorate of the great Village Church in Northbrook, Illinois. Cal says, "After I had been there a few months, a member of the church asked to meet with me. He wanted to know more about the goals in ministry I was bringing to the church. Our schedules didn't mesh and we could not see their doing so for several days. In light of that I suggested he go with me to an Evanston hospital so that we could talk along the way. He agreed. On the way to the hospital we discussed subjects of general interest.

"The patient we went to see was Mary Clark

who just a few weeks before, while sitting in the worship service, had experienced a marvelous new birth in Christ. With tears of joy and a radiant face she had said to me at the door that morning, 'I will never be the same again.' It was true. All who knew Mary saw her life grow in Christ's direction. It was beautiful.

"Mary was in the hospital for the removal of a tumor. She greeted us with a bright, happy face. She was absolutely radiant. As we three discussed the impending surgery Mary said, 'I don't know what tomorrow will bring, but I hope good news. I love life and want to live.'

"She turned to my friend and said, 'But, if not, I am ready to die. I have entered into a whole new life,' then went on to say, 'I have been a member of the Village Church for twenty-two years. I knew about Jesus Christ, but I never knew Him as my Savior and Lord until just a few weeks ago.'" She continued to speak graciously in a most loving manner.

"The three of us joined hands and prayed together. Something of Mary's new faith and joy invaded us. We left her room, and walked a bit in silence. We paused at a point, my friend looked at me, smiled and said, 'I guess that is what ministry is all about, isn't it?' I replied, 'I believe it is.' We rode home in affirmation."

Time together in ministry helps a person sense just what ministry really is. If you have a ministry to visit those who are shut in, don't go alone! Take someone along with you. If you are an usher or a Sunday school teacher, ask someone to join if only for one Sunday. If they say, "I'm not interested in that!" you reply, "Just come be with me. It will give you an opportunity to see what I'm doing." Allow them to experience the joy of ministry without feeling obligated to serve, and you will see them catch their own vision for ministry. Whatever your ministry is, inside or outside of the church, invite someone to be with you.

Jon Story, my backdoor neighbor, likes to tell how one of his good friends, Bob McCallister, was involved with the youth ministry of the Salvation Army. Jon says, "Bob used to drag me down to those meetings. He was using the 'drag me' principle! At first I did not want to go because I didn't want to get involved. But I went simply because I was Bob's friend. I saw the deep needs those kids had and I became interested in them myself." Jon went on to become a deacon in the church whose primary assignment was ministry to the youth of the Salvation Army!

Including people in your ministry is a matter of becoming aware of opportunities in which you might legitimately include another person. Often we do things alone, but with a little effort could involve other people. Hoyt Byrum was invited by David Rule, a Presbyterian pastor in Appalachia, to spend a week as a guest of his church, offering ministry to the church and to the surrounding region of Appalachia. Hoyt might have been tempted to accept the invitation and go alone, but he asked if it would be all right if he brought someone along. David agreed, and Hoyt took Jim Walker, one of the high school seniors from the youth group for which he was responsible. That week of fellowship bonded those men together so closely that years later when Jim had grown up and was married, he and his wife were leading the youth ministry of their church. God used that time not only to knit those two men together in friendship, but to deeply build Jim in his faith in Christ, and in his heart for ministering to youth.

I was asked to moderate a congregational meeting for a church seeking to call a new pastor. It was located about an hour's drive from my home. I called Mike McIntire, a fellow participant in a Bible study with me, and asked if he would be interested in going along for the ride. Obviously, he would have no official role since I was going on behalf of the Presbytery for a very specific function, but it would afford us a great opportunity to talk. He was willing, and we had a great morning together talking about the intellectual basis of the Christian faith (which interests us both deeply). We were able to talk about the whole dynamic by which churches call pastors. It was a great time for us to grow in our friendship with each other and to be in the service of Christ.

When you involve people in a ministry you already have, two things happen: you will deepen your personal friendship, and you will share a vision for ministry. I encourage you to examine the aspects of your personal ministry whether you are a pastor or a church member. Look for those things you do in which you might include other persons. When you invite them, you may hear, "But I don't want to be a Sunday school teacher," or "I don't want to be an usher," or "I'm not interested in hospital visitation," and so forth. To such a concern simply respond, "I am only asking you to spend time with me. It will give you a chance to see what I am doing and it will give us a chance to grow in our friendship." God will use the time to build your friendship, your discipleship, and your mutual heart for ministry to others.

Discussion Questions

1. What ministry responsibility do you have now? It might be "formal" ministry like pastor, teacher, usher, committee person, elder, or deacon. It might be "informal" as you do some volunteer work or lend a helping hand to someone, or visit a person who is ill or shut in.

2. When you do that ministry, who or how many people are with you because of your invitation?

3. How could you include people in your ministry? What invitation on your part will be required?

4. Whom will you ask to join you in the coming week, and for what activity?

Chapter 10

STRENGTHENING YOUR FELLOWSHIP

Imagine being a part of a group that has a great spirit, in which there is a general sense of excitement about what the group is doing. You know many people in the group personally and have an important role within the group. You'd really feel a part of that group, wouldn't you?

If fellowship means "with" at its deepest level, then building the fellowship of any group or church is an essential practice of discipling.

We build fellowship as we help a person "fit" among God's people, when we help them find their niche and feel a part. In essence, we glue—we bond them to the group, in the sense that they are really no longer only an individual—a "me"—but rather part of the "us."

The apostle Peter says that we are all living stones "being built up as a spiritual house" (1 Peter 2:5), and Paul says that we have been, "built upon the foundation of the apostles and prophets, Christ Jesus Himself being the corner stone" (Eph. 2:20). The sense is that we are individual stones in a living temple and that we must fit together. When Paul says that we are being fitted together, one has the sense that each of us as a stone is being chipped and shaped to fit among the people around us. Fellowship is not merely being with a person in the same room, but actually living our lives together in such a way that we build one another, that we belong to one another, and that we are crucial to the support and structure of one another's lives.

Strangely enough, personal relationships within a group can be simultaneously a source of great blessing to the group and a source of real danger. Nothing helps a person feel more included than to know others personally within a group—that's the blessing. But as a person develops a few deep relationships, the time that person has for new relationships begins to diminish. As that happens to person after person within the group, the group as a whole becomes less receptive to new people.

In a sense, an existing group develops a kind of people-blindness. I was talking to my son Lee one day, and he said, "Dad, I don't think I want to play baseball this summer." When I asked him why, I discovered the real reason was that he didn't feel included in a group of other classmates. Upon further questioning, I discovered that the group of his classmates usually ate together at the end of one table and he usually ate alone across the room.

I said, "You know, Lee, when people get in a group, it's like they're blind."

He said, "You mean, they can't see?"

I said, "Well, they can see with their eyes, but it's like they're blind to other people. Instead of seeing you because you're not in the group, they only see each other. If you want to be in that group, you're going to have to invite yourself in. Just go sit with them, and after a while you'll feel a part."

It turned out that that group of boys always rushed to the front of the line and found their place in the cafeteria first. Lee learned to join them in that mad rush out of the room, and was soon a part of the group.

It's so easy for a new person entering a group to feel that that group is not warm, is not hospitable, and has no place. The truth is the group may be quite warm and hospitable from the inside, but because people are blind inside of a group, they really don't have what Chuck Miller calls "people eyes." People eyes are the eyes of Jesus Christ for people. They "see" people who are outside the group or who are new to a group, and seek to help the people feel included in the group. When a group is "people blind," it has replaced people with "program eyes." The people come solely to attend the program. When group members have people eyes, they will seek to minister to the needs of each person working to pull people into the group.

Some time ago I led the founding of a collegiate ministry that has ministered in the lives of thousands of collegians over the years. Recently I went on a winter retreat with about a hundred collegians. Lunch had come, and people were sitting down around tables when the phone rang. The call was for me. After I finished the conversation and had hung up the phone, I walked back into the cafeteria and discovered that every single table was full. Every chair was taken. Here I was, one of the people to begin this fellowship. I had been associated with these collegians for ten years, and yet the way I reacted surprised even me. I was hurt. I felt left out. I felt that nobody loved me, because there wasn't a place for me. Somehow I knew in my own mind that it was absurd, that all I had to do was get a chair and pull it up, but still I felt left out. I actually went so far as to walk out of the room, feeling isolated. Then my own better judgment took over. I went back to the cafeteria, pulled up a chair, and had a great time.

You know, if it's possible for a person who began a group and who has known the people in the group for years to step into the group and feel somehow not a part, somehow not accepted, somehow a stranger, imagine how much more difficult it is for a real stranger, a real new person, to enter into the sense of oneness that the group shares. Although it's proper that we would expect people to have the initiative and the boldness to pull up a chair and to join a table as I eventually did, the reality is that most people don't feel free to do that. If you want the unity that exists within your fellowship to be shared with others, if you want your fellowship to draw others, then you'll have to consciously make inclusiveness, that is, having the people-eyes to welcome new people among you, a major aspect of your emphasis and teaching.

The fact is we're comfortable in existing relationships. Being together is a blessing that can become almost too comfortable. So we have this ongoing and never-ending tension between the comfort of existing friendships and the need to include others, to build new relationships, and to pull people in. There are many ways you can help a fellowship to do this—by encouraging people in your teaching and in your emphases to include others, by enabling many small groups to form within the fellowship in such a way that people are forced to be together on a personal level.

We once took a videotape camera to a large Bible study I teach. The camera was not aimed at me although most of the people thought so, but rather upon the people themselves. We were especially interested in seeing who talked to whom before the formal period of teaching began and afterward as people prepared to leave. It was no surprise for us to discover that most people talked mostly to personal friends. What was surprising was the realization that most of those friends came from the small group Bible studies in which they participated together. We realized that whereas the small group is an essential means of building the Christian faith and life of a person, we needed to make conscious effort to help members of the group focus on people outside of their own group.

Since any group can become a clique when its members focus exclusively on each other and are blind to those on the outside, we look for ways to help people focus outside of their group. One approach that we have found very useful, especially for small groups, is the concept of "ministry in public—friendship in private." When we are meeting as a small group, we focus on each other and enjoy each other's company, and between small group meetings, we can phone each other and spend time together. However, when the members of our small group are in public, as during a worship service in church or a social gathering, we choose to intentionally focus on other people although hellos and brief conversation with people we know well are appropriate, of course. We don't need to focus on each other because we know we will get together again anyway. We work to focus on building new relationships, not merely reinforcing old ones.

You can also encourage true fellowship by fostering a spirit of hospitality in which people within the group invite on their own initiative not only people they know well, but also new people into their homes for a meal. As you make it a message and offer methods by which people can build friendships, the overall web of relationships within the fellowship will grow in health and maturity.

Discussion Questions

1. Have you ever felt you didn't "fit" in a group? How did you feel? What happened?

2. Have you ever been "on the outside" in a group and sensed people's blindness to outsiders? How did it feel?

3. Have you ever been the insider who was blind? Can you recall such an incident?

4. How could your group use the expression, "ministry in public—friendship in private?"

5. How can you help people "fit" into your group?

Chapter 11

KEEPING BALANCE

Is it possible to have too much togetherness? Now that's a good question! I recall a comment by Howard Hendricks to the effect that we cannot be good with people if we are always with people! If the with-me principle means always being among people, physically together, in personal presence, in conversation, in activity—then, of course, we can have too much with-ness. All of us have a need to be alone, to be apart. We need time to center down, to focus on Jesus, to think, to pray, to read, to simply be. Of course, some of us need more time alone than others, but all of us need it. In fact, it is probable that the person who cannot be alone or will not be alone is seeking to compensate for some inner insecurity by means of continual involvement with others. Maturity requires the balancing of time alone and time with others. The biblical concept of withness, of course, goes beyond the idea of being near each other physically. In accord with the concept of *koinonia*, it means shared life. What I have is yours, what you have is mine. We belong together. We are an *us in covenant and in commitment.*

It is appropriate as I grow in Christ to share more of myself with you, both in terms of my material possessions and my inner thoughts, feelings, and concerns. Yet, it is crucial to realize that life is not whole in this life. I do not achieve or receive perfection on earth. There is a need for us to guard certain portions of our inner self. Often, it is only with a deeply trusted person or close friend of the heart that we can appropriately share our deepest concerns, needs, and feelings. Christian maturity recognizes that if I refuse to share myself in terms of possessions or feelings or thoughts, then I limit the extent to which I will be able to grow with others in Christ. On the other hand, we are not called to be excessively vulnerable and transparent to just anyone and everyone. Maturity finds the balance point.

At the root of the with-me principle is the matter of personal courage, the willingness to take a risk to invite others to join us, because as we take a risk we trust God by faith to be at work. We are relying upon His power to fit us person with person and person in group.

An interesting use of this principle is the idea of reversing it. To "reverse" it I seek to be near someone else I know will challenge and help me in my own spiritual journey. As a graduate student at Purdue I used to ask Jim Tozer if I could go with him when he visited in the hospitals. It wasn't the hospitals that interested me, it was the time with Jim that was special. Special moments with Dick Halverson, Chuck Miller, Elton Trueblood, and others significant in my life have occurred because of an opportunity that opened in which I was able to say, "May I be with you?" and they said, "Yes." If there is a person whom you want to get to know as a friend or who will stretch you spiritually, you can certainly reverse the with-me principle and seek that person's company. God will use you in each other's lives.

One of the most life-changing uses of the with-me principle is "with me in a small group Bible study." When you ask others to join with you for a weekly Bible study in a home, many wonderful things happen. You will grow as personal friends as you share life experiences together. You will share personal and spiritual things that will deepen your friendship and stimulate your spiritual growth. Your group will become a source of strength from which you are sent to minister in your world. Thus, the group will help you grow in friendship, discipleship, and apostleship.

As Christ came to break down the dividing wall between people and to bring about unity, so we are to build oneness as members of His Body (Eph. 2, 4). I urge you to invite others to join you in life opportunities that come your way. Look for the moments when you may share personal things and spiritual things. Watch God using your initiative and invitation to build friendships and spiritual growth into your life and into the lives of many others.

Discussion Questions

1. What do you see as the blessings of with-ness? Fellowship as shared life has no limit to its depth. How do you react to the concept of too much togetherness?

2. Intentionally asking people to join you takes courage. How can you develop your courage and begin building more people to be with you?

3. With whom might you "reverse" the with-me principle as a challenge to your spiritual growth?

4. Are you in a small group Bible study? If not, how could you go about starting one or joining one?

EPILOGUE

I hope that you will use the with-me principle to grow as friends with other people and to help each other grow spiritually as well. Perhaps, however, your greatest need right now is for others to welcome you into their lives. We all need to be included, to feel that we fit, to know that other persons want us to be with them. Remember that Jesus Christ, who used the with-me principle two thousand years ago, still uses it today. As the letter to the Hebrews says, "Jesus Christ is the same yesterday and today and forever" (Heb. 13:8 NIV).

The ministry of invitation of Jesus was, "Come to Me all who are weak and heavy laden and I will give you rest." His invitation to you is exactly the same! "Come!" To say yes to the invitation of Jesus Christ is to say yes to the new life He offers, yes to the security and the significance that He alone can give, and to say yes to eternal life. It is to say yes to life itself!

You can respond to the invitation of Jesus Christ by praying a simple prayer: "Lord, Jesus Christ, I want to say yes to You. I want to follow you and to be with you as a child of God. I turn from myself, from my sin, from my own plan for my life, and turn to you as Savior and Lord. I look forward to getting to know you as a friend, becoming like you as your disciple, and being sent to minister to others as your 'apostle.' I look forward to receiving your strength and your guidance this and every day."

If you pray that prayer or one like it, then you can be confident that Jesus Christ is with you according to the promise of His Word, for He keeps His promises. To grow to know Him more deeply, I encourage you to read the gospel of John and to ask the Holy Spirit to help you understand who Jesus Christ is, why He came, and how you can grow as His friend and disciple.

Every man,
I will go with thee,
And be thy guide.
In thy most need,
To go by thy side.